T0159810

THE THREADBARE COAT

Thomas A Clark lives in a small fishing village on the east coast of Scotland. Three earlier books of poetry, published by Carcanet, explore the landscape and culture of the highlands and islands, while numerous small books, cards and editions from his own Moschatel Press investigate ways that the presentation of poetry can inform sense and nuance. Away from the printed page, Thomas A Clark's spare textual interventions attempt to bring imaginative space to public or domestic situations. During the summer months, with the artist Laurie Clark, he runs Cairn Gallery, a space for minimal and conceptual art.

Matthew Welton is the co-editor, with John Lucas, of the *Selected Poems of Nicholas Moore* (Shoestring Press, 2014), and between 2001–2003 was an editor of *Stand* magazine. He has published four books of his own poems with Carcanet, and his pamphlet *Squid Squad* (2016) was published by Thomas A Clark's Moschatel Press. Matthew Welton lives in Nottingham and teaches at the University of Nottingham.

The Threadbare Coat

Selected Poems

THOMAS A CLARK

edited by

MATTHEW WELTON

CARCANET

First published in Great Britain in 2020 by
Carcanet
Alliance House, 30 Cross Street
Manchester M2 7AQ
www.carcanet.co.uk

A CIP catalogue record for this book is
available from the British Library.
ISBN 978 1 78410 998 1

Cover drawing © Laurie Clark
Book design by Andrew Latimer
Printed in Great Britain by SRP Ltd, Exeter, Devon

The publisher acknowledges financial
assistance from Arts Council England.

CONTENTS

SOME THOUGHTS ON FORM

[1]

The idea that poetic form might be a kind of totality seems to apply especially well to the poetry of Thomas A Clark. While his poems make use of traditional elements of poetic structure, such as line, stanza, and rhythm, much of the form comes out of the language. In this, phrasing, syntax and vocabulary seem particularly important.

If it is common to think of the aggregate of technical aspects as constituting a poetic voice, with Clark it is a voice which brings texture to whichever songs it is singing.

[2]

There are a number of words that recur from poem to poem. The hills, clouds and water give us a sense of where we are in the landscape. And the mentions of nothingness, aloneness and longing, say something of what we can expect from territory of this kind.

Sometimes a repeated word can feel like a trusted part of the toolkit. Where 'distance' reappears it brings to the poems depths of different kinds:

> when visitors come
> from their own distance
> there is no one home
>
> [*with*]

blue smoke and distance
are the syllables of her name

        [sonnets]

and one who was passing by
has been detained by distances
that might be heights or depths
earth, water, air or fire
in a break on a stretch of moor

        [at dusk & at dawn]

This combination of adaptability and reliability in certain elements of the vocabulary amount to a kind of fidelity between the poet and the language.

Similarly, the reuse of a limited vocabulary across a range of poems feels appropriate to the landscapes that are the focus of these poems. The shifts in the particulars are part of a larger, continuing experience.

[3]

Another example of a repeated word is 'ripple'. Where it is used to create a similar image in different poems, its repetition conveys both the familiarities of the things of the world and the freshness of each instance in which a thing might be encountered:

the ragwort is rippling

        [floating island]

yellow ragwort rippling in the sunlight

        [the threadbare coat]

Where it is applied in different contexts – as the movement of water, fields, and sound – it brings out the things different things have in common:

> barley combed by the wind/ ripples with warm light
> *[the high path]*

> all the little sounds that come to you sharply, rippling over stillness and cold
> *[the threadbare coat]*

These reused words contribute to the formal effect in each poem they're used in. But they also nudge us to think of the way form might extend across a fuller body of work. They become part of what is going on.

[4]

It may be that the function of the language in a poem is not to say or do whatever the poet wills of it. But through attending to the words as an artist might attend to the paints, brushes and canvas, the poet creates poems that do whatever they have to. Attention is an important part of this.

Gather some of the adjectives from the poems, and the pattern that emerges suggests a continuing interest in the kinds of things that may often be overlooked:

> light, short, small, half-articulated, quiet, few, thin, implied

The title *The Threadbare Coat* – taken from the title of a traditional fiddle tune – is in keeping with this. The focus on what is small or impoverished isn't ever pejorative. In finding a richness in the smallness of things – the beauty in the rough and ramshackle – these poems open themselves to something persistently joyful.

[5]

The nouns are also a vital aspect of these poems' form. The names of plants and birds are a common feature – yarrow, furze, heather; herons, grouse, curlews – as is the use of Scottish place names as the titles of poems – *by kilbrannan sound; coire fhionn lochan*. For these reasons Clark's poems have been seen as a kind of nature writing.

Often, though, these concrete nouns feel as if they are doing something more generic. The paths could be any paths; the meadows could be any meadows. If you tried to use this book as a map you couldn't be certain of where it would get you.

[6]

This effect is strengthened by the frequency of abstract nouns. The relation between the generic objects and the abstraction is a kind of shading.

> when you sail past the islands of the sea
> lean nonchalantly on the rail
> and lose yourself in looking
> at the rocks, the facts, the desolation
> > [*the threadbare coat*]

The texture arises from these shifts, which have the effect of unifying the language and of creating a continuum between concrete and abstract. The sea feels like the idea of the sea; the facts and the desolation feel as tangible as the islands.

[7]

Regular stanzas may be so conventional as to feel almost unnoticeable. This quatrain from *the lord of the isles* shows something characteristic of the stanza in Clark's poems.

as if a thought took hold of them
swarms of flies rise
from salt-tolerant flora
from ranks of rotting weed

As poetic form, this feels unobtrusive. There is enjambment between the lines though the breaks are not abrupt. Yet while the rhythm feels like something at ease and the register is natural enough, these elements combine with such regularity as to make this kind of stanza feel recognizably Thomas A Clark.

[8]

The absence of punctuation in many of these poems feels like a quietly radical private tradition. Without punctuation, the reader has to look around and take in the terrain, and to figure out what goes with what. The path the language takes is clear enough as to make such signposting unnecessary. The reader's alertness to the poem continues the poet's alertness to the world.

[9]

It is notable that 'you' is the prevalent pronoun here. It is a small yet significant step that distances the poems from the 'I' of lyric poetry.

The shift feels not so much romantic as reasonable, and can be startlingly liberating. It means the poems are not tied to Thomas A Clark as a protagonist. He might be talking to himself or addressing a companion, but mostly it helps put the reader into the centre of the action. It is 'you', the reader, who walks up a hill or is standing by a loch.

[10]

The short and very short poems here feel like continuations of the innovations of concrete poetry. Sometimes a short poem might feel like the product of long, steady attention:

> the green of winter jasmine
> awaits the yellow of the flower
>
> the yellow of the flower completes
> the green of winter jasmine

And while there is something conceptual in these symmetrical or permutational poems, in their brevity they offer a kind of delight. In this poem, 'of' is a junction at which changes take place. The nouns are the constants, and the colours their variable properties

[11]

Influence could be seen as a formal element here too. There are three poets a generation older than Thomas A Clark whose work has been important in how Clark's poems have found their shape.

Ian Hamilton Finlay provided an example of how making poems might be a means of investigation of form and presentation, often going beyond what most publishers would allow. His Wild Hawthorn Press was the model for Clark's own Moschatel Press.

The influence of Lorine Niedecker's comes from her approach to the small, carefully crafted poem made of plain language, with a hint of folk song. In conventional terms, it is Niedecker's influence that feels strongest here.

Frank Samperi is an important third influence. His ability to build up a large sequence with small, stand-alone poems, using a lot of space around them – a life's work as an enquiry or vision discovered across individual ordinary incidents – has set the pattern that many of Thomas A Clark's poems have followed.

[12]

It would also be possible to think of Clark's poetic practice as an aspect of form. This feels like another kind of fidelity. This is inventive work, yet it is doesn't have a sensibility that seeks tireless reinvention. The moments that are the poems' focus are ordinary but deserving of our attention. In allowing the curiosity to find something to say, and a way in which to say it, these poems make their discoveries.

Matthew Welton
2020

THE THREADBARE COAT

paths & fruits

to set out early
   with no destination
with the gorse in flower
   with perhaps a light rain

to take the short path
   towards delight or harm
the beards of the ripe barley
   caressing your bare arm

to wander, linger
   digress and forget
to be full in response
   to be able to wait

to waste time watching
   raindrops in a pool
make small circles lasting
   no time at all

to approximate less
   to oak and rock
than to air, mist
   water, smoke

to talk and to listen
   and to turn on your heel
to steady yourself
   on the curve of the hill

to work again at your own
   half-articulated tune
to be as glad in the rain
   as a mountain burn

to sleep in the sunshine
   a sleep as light as air
to be alone and lonely
   for a mile or more

to go on and on
    expecting nothing
to be everywhere transparent
    displacing nothing

to feel while the wind
    howls over stones
or tears at the meadow grasses
    quiet in your bones

to pause before entering
    a stand of trees
to splash your face with water
    and then lift it to the breeze

to slowly unravel
    the knots of desire
that bind up distances
    of cold and fire

to take the stile
   beside the open gate
that leads to a profusion
   of flowers and light

to leap across the waters
   of a swift-flowing stream
to sit beside it, to step
   in and out of time

to clear a small space
   between stimulus and response
to stare into the haze
   and watch an oak tree dance

to detach yourself from
   each form and event
until the days take on
   depth, clarity, extent

by kilbrannan sound

the glare of a black stone

the gleam of a black stone

the glimmer of a black stone

the glint of a black stone

the glitter of a black stone

the gloss of a black stone

the gloom of a black stone

the glow of a black stone

thainig na naoi sonais
le na naoi marannan

came the nine joys
with the nine waves
with the nine joys
of the nine waves
and the nine waves
of the nine joys

creag liath

island of many inlets
shape bitten by the tide
little bays in which to linger
spray reaching to its shoulder

a few strides east to west
out of kilter south to north
island of peaks and corries
remote, bright, various

its obscurity lifting into clarity
a lonely place to be alone
sunbeams sharpened on its ridges
acid water in rock pools

it is a place apart, grey
a thin wedge in blue
where you were left abandoned
by an impulse or a tide

island persisting in itself
drawing the mist about it
firm ground to stand on
in a tilting sea and sky

with hills implied behind cloud
soil impoverished by rain
a few sheep pull at a thin
crop of sedge and drawmoss

island exposed and sheltered
fertile of colours and forms
contained place in which to be
both accurate and expansive

ruined dwellings on open moors
wild goat paths through heather
paths with nowhere to go
where there is nothing to do

among the sedimentary deposits
intrusions of coarse-grained granite
with crystals of amethyst, topaz
blue-beryl, smoky quartz

having rare flowers in profusion
by burns, in flushes, on wet rocks
strewn across meadows, solitary
in crevices, on ridges and crags

with remnants of woodland
birch, rowan and aspen
huddled in ravines
gullies of fern and bracken

a quiet to drive out sense
a wind to lean against
a wind that can drop
to make you doubt your shape

to the east bare and tranquil
shifting dunes to the west
some couch grass to stabilise
peat sweetened with blown sand

sandpiper piping from a stone
lifting and settling on a stone
far cry of a curlew
a corncrake clearing its throat

the hours long and inconsequential
waving glumes of marram grass
the days harsh and tender
primroses in a nest of rock

where strict limits engage
particulars, set at a distance
from distraction and noise
balanced on the crest of a wave

coire fhionn lochan

lapping of the little waves
breaking of the little waves
spreading of the little waves
idling of the little waves

rippling of the little waves
settling of the little waves
meeting of the little waves
swelling of the little waves

trembling of the little waves
dancing of the little waves
pausing of the little waves
slanting of the little waves

tossing of the little waves
scribbling of the little waves
lilting of the little waves
sparkling of the little waves

leaping of the little waves
drifting of the little waves
running of the little waves
splashing of the little waves

sixteen fiddle tunes

get up early
stack the rags
saddle the pony
scatter the mud

take it easy
drive the cows home
wallop the spot
come in from the rain

smash the windows
strike the young harp
wait awhile
don't leave me all alone

fill the cup
hide and go seek
forget not the angel
come to the dance

the high path

   let's take the high path
that clings to the cliff edge
    through the ripe barley
past the corn marigolds
taking up this and that
   dropping this or that

like a rag or a flag
  space flaps in the wind
fluttering and settling
   between scabious
   and knapweed the sea
flutters lightly away

   trust the tangled path
the sea at your elbow
   it will lead you through
complex information
meadow-grass and bent-grass
   to a fine sea view

in among the grasses
   are the manifold
spaces little places
   where intention is
    no longer gathered
but ramified dispersed

   pale comfrey flowers
linger in green spaces
   in the tall bracken
as if such spaces were
formed by bracken for
   pale comfrey flowers

melancholy thistle
   rest harrow, milk vetch
climb through the long grasses
   to add at random
   a touch of colour
to the drift of colours

the waves are dancing
and the light bounces back
   into a larger
atmosphere or climate
that you move in gladly
   in receipt of light

over the tall grasses
   the blue sky stretches
an unimpeded blue
   you can lie back in
   crushed grasses and let
your head fill up with blue

   swallows swooping low
over the ripe barley
   respond as keenly
to the intelligence
as barley to the least
   rumour of a breeze

barley combed by the wind
   ripples with warm light
as if the light were not
   given but contained
   given out when combed
by the light-seeking wind

   the waves of the barley
the ripples of the sea
   flow in or out from
your feet as you pass through
the ripples of the barley
   the waves of the sea

as a hawthorn will show
   the prevailing wind
in a motionless gust
   of whipped-back branches
   you take the shape of
what you know let it go

is it far when you think of it

is it grey when you think of it

is it cold when you think of it

is it clear when you think of it

is it small when you think of it

is it there when you think of it

the far-glimpsed island

the clear-seen island

the mist-veiled island

the wave-rocked island

the spray-washed island

the sun-bathed island

the music of the wind
the fragrance of the pine

the fragrance of the wind
the music of the pine

cumulus nimbus stratus
sandstone basalt granite

about nothing in particular

to make a short song
out of nothing, a few words
to keep me going
to take nothing's notation
is a mile's occupation

the thistle and gorse
the kiss, the blessing, the curse
are built on nothing
the cairn, the old fort, the hill
the tibia of the gull

that water is best
that bubbles up out of rock
tasting of nothing
in a lull in a cold wind
I have stretched out to drink it

convolvulus stems
the complexities of thought
old country dances
weave figures around nothing
bring plenitude from nothing

you are my good friend
the best of company on
the long shore road home
when there is nothing to say
you stay quiet and easy

just before the dawn
I woke to the sound of rain
and knowing nothing
of my location or shape
like the grass I was refreshed

sonnets

I will pick the smooth yarrow
that my voice may be gladder
that my words may be arrows
that my syllables be hard
as tide tossed pebbles
may I be an island in the sea
may blue sea asters cover me
may I leap upon the hillside
I will grasp the spear thistle
that no man shall wound me
may no rumour find me
I will weave the thistledown
I will be a windblown reed
my songs will lure the salmon

our boat touches the bank
among a scent of bruised sedge
the startled heron rises
broken from his austerities
we are in a proud country
where stone chats to stone
where furze pods crackle open
grey grouse and curlews inform
keep well below the horizon
your flesh spare upon the bone
trust to flintlock and sabre
bed down among the heather
the wild fiddle music of the air
tuneless will find you anywhere

when cattle sniff the air
and herd together in corners
rain will invariably follow
when bees fly short distances
dogs lie about the fireside
it is safe to forecast rain
when singing frogs croak when
toads come forth in numbers
it is a certain sign of rain
when swans fly against the wind
it is a sign of coming rain
when moles are more industrious
when worms appear on the surface
one must surely forecast rain

my eyes that were hungry
dwelt gladly on these stones
the stimulus of varied tints
as if when parched with thirst
I had been given a drink
on the monotonously grey sky
there towered a huge cloud
like a smile like a greeting
and I stretched out both hands
towards such colours and forms
I shall send you a line farewell
till we meet in my new prison
the sky and clouds come with me
I shall not take leave of them

a blessing on the house
from flags to roof tree
may its chimney never tremble
may its lintel be confirmed
a tune always in its hearth
brightness in its threshold
may its latch be lifted
may its well never fail
with fresh bread on the table
a health in every glass
a blessing on the host
a blessing on the guest
may there be trust between them
light and shade in their conversation

I will gather the fern seed
to wound me you must find me
am I laughter over water
or a crag above the broom
I will lurk in brightness
my greatcoat will be weather
in the evening and the morning
are you sure I am the same
intelligence and vigilance
will never discover me
I am a rumour over heather
a small compaint in your ear
look for me aside, askance
I am a mist over turbulence

I would not tell her name
for a month of fine mornings
blue smoke and distance
are the syllables of her name
the silver birch and hazel
look dismal beside her
all the tribes of sleet and rain
only make her shine the more
wine laced with pine resin
is not so convivial
a clover or rock pool
is not so self-contained
though the hills were to ask me
I would not tell her name

in blue and in green
in grey-green and blue
leaf-dapple we are falling asleep
in a hammock of hours
with all that is ours
we are falling asleep to sleep
sleep well little strawberry thief
sated with fruit and kisses
let go of the branch
let go of the leaf
we are falling falling asleep
in a solace of shadow
with head upon hip
we are falling falling a

graveyard by the sea

far out on the headland
there is a graveyard by the sea
where a few carved stones
lean among uncarved stones

the waves play around it
seals come in to enquire
the dead are glad to sleep here
ragwort nodding in the sunlight

the rippling of the waves
does not disturb them
the sparkling of the waves
does not delight them

fathers and daughters
mothers and sons
fishermen and weavers
smugglers and idlers

the poorest graves are marked
with uncarved stones
inserted roughly into the earth
as if dropped from a cloud

mothers and daughters
fathers and sons
pipers and fiddlers
preachers and rievers

who went out and in
who knew each rock by name
who spun the long stories
who breathed on the embers

out of the sweet light
far from praise and blame
retired from the loom
lazy the long day

at every moment another
impression escapes them
a sense in the stream
of moments escapes them

who gathered the wind
who drove the tractor
to herd the sheep
who walked by the tide

the gorse and the broom
will blossom without them
the blackthorn will turn
white without them

they have nothing to say
let's leave a pause
at the end of the line
to listen in

habits are dissolved in air
kindness to strangers
cries of girls and curlews
personal graces in air

flushes of melt water
strategies of evasion
peat and haar and smoke
distilled to spirit

from bryophytes to butterflies
whatever enjoys the privilege
of moving or perceiving
explores the privilege

anything under the sun
everything above the earth
dances in celebration
of old time dancers

the fort of stillness

the approach is oblique
a clattering stone
set into the causeway
gives notice of intrusion

no remains of a doorway
can be verified
the defences are
now inconspicuous

where the walls
have disappeared
they must be
inferred

round an interior space
for the most part indistinct
the foxglove is abundant
the rare wild rose

the quiet island

then we came to a quiet island
   where waves dropped quietly on the shore
where streams flowed quietly and waterfalls
   poured silence
we spoke there in whispers
   and a rumour ran through the reeds
that quiet was healing
   that quiet would heal our wounds
dawn spread dusk settled
   the interior of the island was quiet
you could lean back into quiet
   you could carry it about
the cock didn't crow the bull didn't bellow
   dogs had lost their bark
the woods were great reserves of quiet
   the hills were resting bells

soon we had had enough of it
    but were too polite to say
that quiet needs interruption
    that events are a melody
branches were heavy with moss
    apples dropped without sound
you could glean the sweet
    bruised fruits of quiet
you could spread your bread with honey
    from the quiet hive
mountains were wrapped in mist
    rocks in wool
hollows filled with pollen
    the days were thistledown
on a morning early we went down to the sea
    and pushed the boat out
quietly

some details of hebridean
house construction

the walls are built with
unmortared boulders
the external faces having
an inward slope
the corners rounded

roofs are thatched with
straw, ferns or heather
and weighted with stones
hung from heather ropes

instead of overhanging
the roof is set back
on a broad wall-top
which in the course of time
becomes mantled with
grass and verdure
which may provide
occasional browsing
for a sheep or goat

back to the wind
face to the sun
is the general
orientation

the floor is of beaten earth
and the main room is reached
by way of the byre
there are no windows and
the frugal flame of the peat
gives the only illumination
smoke wanders and finds
egress by a hole in the roof

in the outer isles the floor is covered
with white sand from the machair

a few steps ascend
the wall near the door
to enable the roof
to be thatched or roped
or the family to sit
in the summer weather
and sew, chat or knit

by the peat store
near to the doorway
is placed a large stone
for the wanderer to sit on

the earthly paradise

not on this island

not on that island

not on this island

not on that island

not on this island

string

ropes of heather
weighted with stones
to anchor a thatch
of rushes and heather

a white plastic bag
flapping in the wind
to scare the birds
from a string of fish
drying in the sun

a string plucked to leave
a line of yellow chalk

for clematis
and vine
green twist
two ply
garden twine

the ampersand is a knot
tying two parts of a discourse
sea & land
adventure & homecoming
subject & object

if you pull on it
everything that is
attached to it
will come with it

when you are hopeful
you are still the boy
who stood by the burn
hopefully, a hook
at the end of a string

saxifrage & campion
rock & torrent
loss & consolidation

with reef knots
with draw knots
tied to you

tied to you
with slip knots
with clove hitch

every tug on the rope
only tightens the splice

whatever is wrapped
in paper and string
may be unwrapped
from string and paper

blackbirds have stolen
the coloured twine
you tied round
the rowan saplings

green & yellow

the green of winter jasmine
awaits the yellow of the flower

the yellow of the flower completes
the green of winter jasmine

the little *loch* of the trout
the little loch of the *trout*
the *little* loch of the trout
the little loch *of* the trout

under the twists of water
among the pondweed
the slender naiad
among the duckweed
under the braids of water

a
thin
   trickle
of
   water
through
   the
watercress
   is
enough

of woods & water
(forty eight delays)

on a wide bend of the river
there is a leisurely turning of water
that flows so profoundly it can
relax into every gesture

a mist rising from water
drifts grey over green
a slow mist of willows
pale green over green

on the edge of a wood
a moment's hesitation
how will you conduct yourself
in the company of trees

willow branches spread and fall
around a space that holds the air
or detains it while it comes and goes
within a room whose walls are leaves

mist is gathered by leaves
to fall as rain beneath the trees
with a sound that will not carry
beyond the edge of the wood

drip drip of raindrop
under alder under willow
dissonances little distances
briefly there or here

the broad beech branches
are darker in the rain
and the lichens on the branches
are a deeper green

a dark slow-moving water
combs the water-crowfoot
long currents of water-crowfoot
turning in the twists of water

the water as it slows
through watercress discovers
the calm of a completed form
to ripple away from

roots wrapped in moss
lightly the beech trees tread
on the soft ice-broken earth
where they pause, is a wood

holding you here
leading you there
the song of a blackbird
the prints of deer

small birds in the branches
bullfinch chaffinch warbler
these names are wrong
small birds in the branches

lighter than birds
moving through branches
the shadows of birds
moving through branches

more light on the branch
more light on the leaf
than appears to fall
on branch or leaf

fresh water continually
flowing into fresh water
barely disturbing the surface
and slipping imperceptibly away

after the shower
it goes on raining
gently on the pond
under the willow

the falling light defines
tall regions in the air
to shrug from your shoulders
as you push through them

beneath a tracery of branches
it seems that something is there
that a few steps might take you
to what the branches defer

shade is the candour
of a modest revelation
an immediacy hidden
in continual mediation

the sound of water flowing
resourcefully over roots and stones
rises through layers of foliage
in little snatches and runs

trembling of the leaves
trembling of the water
trembling of the light
thrown back by water

green filling every distance
taking up all of your vision
now temperate now radiant
green dipped in the stream

in this tree shining
in that branch glowing
now in this place
now in that place

in the green each incident
of yellow blue or pink
is temporal or spatial
a note or a tone

what you thought might take place
is what thought will displace
the trace of a presence
a thrill through the grass

the prepositions
in under through
before behind among
the propositions

across the intricacy
of scrub an intensity
of effect or affect
flickers briefly

the grace of the birch belongs to it
it is not the gift of a passing breeze
is there a shape you recover again
when what moves you leaves you

you will have to walk
all round it to see it
you will have to stay
with it to know it

something made of shadow
at the edge of attention
with an undulating motion
retreats into shadow

little restless or dancing forms
now on the near side of the water
now on the far side of the water
little restless or dancing forms

beneath reflected trees and hills
where a mallard pushes an arc
of light into darkness
a body of water slips away

quiet and song
beech and alder
space and time
lean on each other

the trunk of the birch
pale in the shadows
the crown of the birch
open to the air

the gesture of the birch
turning in the stillness
the leaves of the birch
laid on the air

a broken branch
leaking resin
a wood warbler's nest
of leaf debris and moss

a trace of passage
something dragged through the grass
fallen lintel broken wall
vestige of a stair

push your way in
under through to where
the moss is green
on the given stone

green above you
below and behind you
green with you
green around you

when you come up out
of shadow, for a moment
you are lost, prised open
by light, without content

small bird with a note
like the creaking of a branch
twice the weight of a leaf
lost in leaf dapple

a turbulance in water
is conveyed to the air
coolness moves the willow
and the shadows move

a shift in light
a distribution of shadows
a configuration of shadows
the imputation of a form

in a tangle of scrub
a white calligraphy
its swift notation
scribbled over at a glance

try to listen
farther in to where
in an intimation
no branch breaks

through the complexity
of lichened branches
the lure of a trajectory
you will not take

to go with the stream
or against the stream
to flow away continually
to be constantly replenished

on a wide bend of the river
there is a leisurely turning of water
away from the light and into
a broad course of darkness

hollow

filling with the pollen
of hazel and willow

filling with the pollen
of meadowsweet and mallow

cress & mint

as water through watercress
sense through the line

as water through watermint
sense through the line

the grey plover

the ringing spaces
behind the hills
the bow of the fiddle
draws from the strings

melodeon

the thin organ-like tone
is produced by air
blown across the reeds

willow warbler

then one morning
the song is everywhere
in woods in clearings
in willow or alder

the song is a sweet
descending cadence
not loud but clear
carrying to a distance

it starts up round and full
then runs down the scale
to expire on the air
in a soft murmur

when disturbed flies off
feigning injury
sounding plaintive notes
of anxiety

briefly clinging
to twig or stem
it gently fans
one wing at a time

having sufficient weight
when in flight
to set the green
in modulation

nests

a cup of grass, moss and lichen
in a platform of woven twigs
is placed on the branch of a conifer

shredded wool, green moss
spider silk and lichens
are woven into a dome

all the available space
is filled with grass and moss
lined with wool and feathers

composed of young furze shoots
ling, moss and galium stems
hidden in gorse or heather

materials may include
the hair of red deer, fur of the hare
feathers of grouse or ptarmigan

of blades of sedge or reed
in beds of reed mace or sedge
inches above the water

in a wild rose bush
in elder, thorn or willow
swaying when the wind blows

hidden in winter litter
when bracken fronds unfold
impossible to find

wood warbler

unseen if not heard
a bird of the wood
its slight restless form
barely rippling the calm

a dome of dried grasses
leaf debris and moss
its nest is hidden
among the fronds of bracken

now it sails out with
extended wings and tail
quivering as it descends
in a loose spiral

a few preliminary notes
inserted among
rustling leaves and raindrops
soon quicken into song

a small commotion
in the canopy of oak
it perches shaken
by its own music

when silent unseen
pale yellow and green
in a daze or camouflage
of translucent foliage

of many waters

little swift one
little rough one
little one of virtue
little stony one
little loud one
little herbaceous one
little ember
little rushy one
little one of difficulty
little lasting one
little dry one
little thwart one
little one of alders
little talkative one
little dusky one
little minnow

weasel

the colour of dusk
its belly of dawn
the weasel slips between
tact and discrimination

speed is its rest
with a nip to the base
of the skull it will
pin objects to space

there is a mist
of the faculties
that comes awake
to qualities

blow across a grass blade
like an animal in pain
the sound will bring
shadows to attention

the absence
of a thing
in the presence
of its name

curlew

the absence
of a thing
in the presence
of its name

plover

some smoke

smoke rising through turning light
scent of crushed rosemary and smoke
smoke and wool snagged on wire
old stories told through smoke
smoke screen of old stories
a theft of honey in a puff of smoke
smoke from burning carried away
dusk of loneliness and smoke

the shape changer

once I was a deer
stepping under trees
my form always broken
by lights and shadows

then I was a wildcat
leaping up and away
from the traces of my own
rigour and ferocity

in a fold of hills
nodding with flowers
I took on many
shapes and colours

seldom was I present
to myself in a form
half as alluring
as what I might become

again I was a goldcrest
a bright fragment of song
moving through the forest
leading farther in

at times defeated
reduced to stone
I lay disregarded
concealed in the open

then I was a juniper
turning to take the slope
pausing and bracing myself
above a sheer drop

and once I was a dragonfly
for an afternoon
little more than a notion
of the stillness and the green

sylvidae

to green add green
a shade of brown
shyly
to make a difference slightly
then from green
subtract green

little or nothing
draws the attention
to a thorn where a warbler
drops from a sensible
to a notional branch
from noun to preposition

leaf marsh willow
wood reed sedge
the warblers
light as grasses
swing from the grasses
context their content

a tremor, a lure
was it there or here
attention follows
the least deflection
from the direct line
from the true

in the feathered edges
of perception
a doubt
or hesitation
a heartbeat
away from detection

slender as a leaf
it gleans from the canopy
a gentleness of tone
soft green and yellow
and from shifting light
mobility

to fly, to fall
out of the immediate
into a hush
or ash of shadows
a chiff chaff
of differences

in tussocks of grass
or from a bramble stem
a reportoire of syllables
short and long
a constantly varied
umbellifer of song

to be sheltered
shaded, to be slight
in shabby foliage
in lovely greenness
ramshackle seedhead
shaken by light

a nest of grasses
moments and moss
where residence
is residual
little more than an emphasis
lifted

when the least that might
be added is added
a note to a tone
a shape to a shade
then the least that might
be thought is thought

perhaps the warbler
knows to forget
itself in colours
close to its heart
in a sigh it is
lost to sight

green

will you be vine
sweet briar or vetch

flowers several
leaves radical

the head foliate
the mind green

tendrils from the tear ducts
syllables on the tongue

stubbled with burrs
dappled with shadows

intention branching
to complexity

will you be bindweed
or jack-by-the-hedge

will you be willow
clover or woad

the yellow butterfly

here among some green
words that shade it or
try to avoid it
a butterfly puts
in an appearance

little wandering
yellow butterfly
little tender shock
shade beside green shade
ripples in its wake

it may be the first
yellow broken free
from fruit or flower
to rise to its own
yellow adventure

in the time it takes
to see it it drops
out of sight again
open to vision
closed to inspection

at any moment
it is here or there
this colour this shape
yet makes its escape
through all its moments

pollen that a breeze
shakes out of cedar
is no brighter than
this ragged paper
thrown up by a breeze

if you sit as still
as a green hill slope
resting on water
soon it may flutter
round your empty head

grace is to follow
yellow in a daze
deeper into green
to trust yourself to
an intuition

to give yourself once
to lose yourself twice
to be blown away
lured from intention
by a butterfly

you were a stranger
to the wood walking
carefully through forms
estrangement brought near
to revelation

where green trembles at
the beat of a wing
flight is a constant
setting in motion
of variation

nothing has happened
in going nowhere
yellow in a trance
has traced its absence
in a yellow dance

the grey sallow

on a grey day
in a haze of yellow
you might come upon
the grey sallow

leaves lanceolate
grey-green above
downy beneath
arranged alternately

the grey sallow
is not the sallow
it is not the weeping
or the bay willow

the grey catkins
turn a brilliant gold
covered in flecks
of yellow pollen

a host to bees and moths
to the sallow clearwing
the sallow kitten
the dusky clearwing

when a grey wind blows
through the grey leaves
the tree is restored
to its frailty

along unassuming ways
in the profusion of summer
it holds itself
in reserve

of moist places
in a green hollow
among the stitchwort
by the grey mare

lemna minor

flowers rare
        leaves light green
floating on water

small green ovals
        drift in shoals
in ditches and pools

when ducks push through
        duckweed it floats
in again behind them

an alder leaf
        flutters down
onto green

neat norwegian horizon

spruce

sad scotch horizon

pine

the yellow mist

hazel

a dancer to forgotten tunes

oak

lullaby

in the tall grasses
the night-scented grasses
a warm breath is held
      then exhaled
as pale moths rise

you who hesitate
on the skirts of the wood
you will be one
      and alone when
you slip your solitude

the little commotion
of a bird tumbling
down through light
      let it beat
on your eyelids

my willow of the stream
my berry of the brae
my lapwing of the moor
      in your own care
go lightly

some twists of rope
of heather and smoke
to tie your roof
        while you drift
through storms

curlew and cormorant
the colours of dusk
an arrow of wild geese
        a slow release
of thistledown

the folds of granite
the pillows of lava
the quartz veins
        bedded down
the sediments and deposits

you are falling asleep
bee drone in a foxglove
far movement of the sea
        listen to me
you are falling asleep

by a rill

by a little
            rill
that trickles
            down
a gully from
            a patch
of snow
            on a
shallow
            but moist
and sheltered
            ledge
the tufted
            saxifrage

the threadbare coat

air flows almost continuously
from the sea over adjacent land
moist air blanketing the earth
against heat loss in winter
the climate is mild but severe
on plant growth and livestock
loss of heat from the body
reduces energy and mobility
where a fine wind-borne sand
sweetens the acid of peat
you are smitten with distance
a wound with salt in it

collected on a bright day
from cliffs above the sea
wild honey of the whin
eat it and hunger for it
look for it and find it
for honey of bell heather
take the hives to the moor
or to sheltered tidal margins
to gather from the sea pink
gather pollen from the willow
the sycamore's early nectar
nectar of bramble and clover

when you walk by the sea
the light shifts on the water
attention comes and goes
when you walk by the sea
when you walk by the sea
it waits at your shoulder
it is the same and not the same
when you walk by the sea
when you walk by the sea
the mist tastes of rosemary
your dimensions are variable
when you walk by the sea

in by, behind a broken wall
something torn or discarded
lies among red-stemmed rushes
among hints and water-glints
bog myrtle of the mire
cotton grass of the evening
crows flit from whin to whin
unless arrested by an implication
over there, where outlines blur
in a shimmer of neglect
shapeless, heavy with rain
something lies where it fell

an ointment of buttercups and daisies
is effective for bruises and sores
for listlessness and melancholy
the green root of the sea pink
sanicle is an astringent
comfrey is a knitter of bones
for bee stings and burns
cool damp leaves and fronds
treat sorrow with yarrow
lovage will cure all ills
taking herbs and healing grasses
press them to the hurts and wounds

in intention you leap ahead
losing the road you must travel
the miles are a weariness
the thistle heavy with dust
start again, follow the idle road
that lingers over differences
never arrive before you leave
the clear air is not hung with bells
to bring you back to where you are
it is a task to turn and see
the meadowsweet at your elbow
the blackthorn in the hedge

you will never find a stone
without a place in the world
nor a song with enough weight
to bend a willow branch
you cannot tie a cord
about a shaft of light
nor close the space between
consciousness and self-consciousness
you cannot gather berries
from gorse or broom
nor step across a stile
from evening to morning

when you sail past the islands of the sea
don't flinch, don't turn away
from their complete indifference
it's nothing personal, it's not you
when you sail past the islands of the sea
lean nonchalantly on the rail
and lose yourself in looking
at the rocks, the facts, the desolation
there is no sense in asking
if you see, hear, touch, feel
you slip away, are sadly absent
when you sail past the islands of the sea

an island that dances away
from every approach towards it
an island of sedge and lyme-grass
bright like an open face
an island or glimpse of something
significant but misted over
an island with a boat
pulled up on the shore
an island to which singing voices
come at night over the water
an island of yellow ragwort
rippling in the sunlight

don't look but see
over there under juniper
a flicker or a flutter
where something is withdrawn
don't listen but hear
all the little sounds that come
to you sharply, rippling
over stillness and cold
it is a principle of tact
not to focus, not to bear
down heavily on the evidence
but to hover, vigilant and tender

choose the willow of the stream
the berry from the highest branch
the sloe of the first frost
the event as it happens
choose the hazel of the rocks
the dawning of the day
the wine of the burn
the unfailing remedy
choose the elm of the brae
the primrose of the islands
melody before sense
the high tide alternative

two strangers turned up late
and you gave them shelter
a bite to eat, some strong tea
they said nothing
but went on their way
now your table is spread with light
you have enough and to spare
your mind is sheltered everywhere
lay out bread and milk
wild flowers in a jar
that you may not arrive
a stranger at your own door

flower of the lochan
green one of the wood
little slender one
plant of the virtues
plant of the sharp rocks
wild little aromatic one
little yellow one of summer
food of the prince
plant that staunches bleeding
little bitter one
cress of healing
gift of the sea

if the waves were silver
and the leaves were gold
if the miles were accomplishments
and the hours were joys
you would give them all away
if cares were goods
and moods were faculties
if an impulse brought you to
banks of wild strawberries
you would give them all away
whatever your thought can touch
all that your hands can reach

nine paces

an empty
  ochre-brown
    ice-scoured land

yellow flags
  tall beside
    a green loch

behind cloud
  a mountain's
    implied weight

minnows dart
  through leached peat
  ditch water

an old fort
   defenceless
      against light

in an ache
   of stillness
      moss on stone

perception
   tender as
      primroses

the warm scent
   of a strand
      of snagged wool

breaking ice
  bathe the mist
    from your eyes

water from
  a well in
    a pure land

you were far
  from yourself
    until now

rock burned hands
  cooled in a
    waterfall

showers of
  light shaken
    from cedars

a glow for
  one moment
    on a stone

nine paces
  leading to
    nine places

odd little
  water song
    lost again

a light breeze
  of small birds
    through birch leaves

reflected
  green ripples
    on beech boles

paper boat
  becalmed in
    watermint

the swelling
  note before
    the full song

something slips
  away from
    inspection

little pulse
  in the air
    dying out

a stonechat
  chip chipping
    at silence

a stillness
  littered with
    stripped spruce cones

washing with
   raindrops from
      pine branches

a cold light
   poured over
      the shoulders

the blast from
   a gust of
      goldfinches

one shy high
   stepping through
      tall grasses

thin birch branch
  more lichen
    than birch branch

a terse note
  repeated
    farther in

love shakes you
  like a breeze
    through aspens

broken gate
  reclining
    on brightness

a walk in a water meadow

a walk in a water meadow
among the standing grasses
the mist closing in
sounds dampened down
walking and standing
in disclosed places

by gentleness of circumstance
things come separately
out of the mist
detached from context
nothing seeks its precedent
trying its own weight

fine webs spread
to catch the mist
cotton-grass and cuckoo-spit
deposits of mist
a trout in the current
almost transparent

a walk in a water meadow
among coloured grasses
through drenched grasses
hints and tints and touches
of colour bleeding onto mist
stains and residues

among the floating levels
places are provisional
a drawn breath
a notation of grasses
splinters and ruins
of larch and pine

an impaired vision
peers forward to where
vision will be repaired
as if the mediations
of mist might lead
into the immediate

skeins of mist
snagged on larch
untangled from pine
suspended explorations
of vetch over grasses
circles spreading on water

a breath exhaled
a path erased
separate voices wander
terns dive to sip
at a cream of light
that might be water

sounds dampened down
alders sentinels
over water-locked localities
wrapped in wool
unravelling to reveal
one quality

in a time of mist
a walk in a water meadow
floats and drifts
it arrives and waits
stilling clouded water
mist dropped syllables

wrap yourself in rags
of mist and water
of mint and clover
all that is folded
into grey and silver
will be unfolded later

a walk in mist
makes no progress
history is suspended
resolve dissolves
a tree-creeper creeps into mist
a body of water slips away

a small country

a small country sparsely populated
with a wealth of resources
never exploited
people seldom go far
their boats never venture
far from the shore
they have sophisticated devices
but seldom use them
energy and intelligence
but never display them
well-fed and clothed
living simply and quietly
they are honest to the honest
honest to the less than honest

the fragrant glumes of sweet vernal grass

the silver leaves of blue fescue

the nodding spikes of wild oat

the sharp awns of meadow barley

the sheathed stems of marram grass

the soft panicles of yorkshire fog

the waving plumes of common reed

the swollen fruits of yellow sedge

sweet vernal grass

sweet vernal grass

sweet vernal grass

sweet vernal grass

sweet vernal grass

cowberry cranberry
crowberry blueberry
delicious little
differences
bilberry blaeberry
blackberry bramble

from a grey notebook

along a lonely shore
one curlew

as if you were implicated
mist lifts from the water

content is an emergent
property of context

on rocks at the tide's edge
lift your wings to dry

vestigial birchwood
peat-buried pine

all the means of filling time
emptied out again

folded arms have the gravity
of folded rocks

a yellow butterfly can visit
the ruins of an old fort

gabbro with dykes of basalt
great collapse of shale

dry flush and damp flush
mountain top detritus

bog moss and cotton grass
rush moth and moor rush

an ease you recognise
stumbled into by surprise

the birch trees are quiet
as you walk up through them

cup marks in stone
fill with rain

rills and torrents
send voices down the rocks

you are quiet coming down
through the birch trees

in a monotone of green
go on and on

fragrance is the remnant
of an ancient forest

shredded light
waxwing songs

not a flicker of thought
without a redistribution

tall thin things
stand in the rain

a note like two stones
struck lightly together

immediacy may be
leisurely

the pollen of the meadow
the dust of the road

water rushes past
glades where sunlight rests

oak trees are appropriate
among rocks

the burn of sorrow
meets the burn of care

floating leaves propose
order to fluidity

a ridge of limestone
a shelf for colours

coming down to the water's edge
remembering an old tune

these are the wagtail days
that skim the surface

born from thunder
damselfly

a pause on the hill slope
a rest in music

continuity is sketched
across its interruptions

lean on the wind
but not too far

if you tumble down the hill
the sky will tumble with you

stones that were walls
return to stones

overgrown with angelica
red-currant in profusion

to each a portion of land
each with its portion of rain

you do not know the words
that will shelter you

great lifting wings beating
great beating wings lifting

in space and time and rain
chewing a sorrel leaf

everything you have lost
goes with you

the melancholy thistle
of the roadside verges

there are fires that outlast
those who tend them

in the gloom the sparks
fly upward

in the stillness of the night
the crack of burning branches

with sepia ink write
in the grey notebook

the lord of the isles

small high islands lying
somewhere to the west
approach them in feeling
touch them in thought

missing real objects
set in wine-dark quantities
basalt and granite
perpetually perishing

but for the songs of birds
the cries of waders
you might miss them in the mist
you might miss them

cereals in the pollen record
depredations of sheep and goats
postglacial drift of peoples
decline in elm and lime

winds lift long veils
of spindrift from breakers
move sand from the shallow
offshore shelf to the beach

sands of pure quartz
basalt sands and coral sands
sea meadows of machair
thickets of yellow iris

adumbrations of islands
saturated with assumptions
acres of ochre
untrampled heather

strands of seaweed move in a wave
in response to a shifting impulse
backward and forward and back
mats of seaweed on a wave

dark islands bright seas
opaque or translucent forms
unmoored from time
geologically young

saltings pink with thrift
with glasswort and sea milkwort
give densely grazed pasture
for sheep and for thought

indigenous mice
indigenous sheep and wren
melanic lepidoptera
cryptic on resting surfaces

as if a thought took hold of them
swarms of flies rise
from salt-tolerant flora
from ranks of rotting weed

sweet scent of sea campion
languor of the afternoon
on eventful days
their influence is dimmed

for a rent of gannet feathers
hectares of grasses and sedges
to be held at a distance
in perpetuity

under slabs of pink granite
small fry in pools
moved by a shadow
dart between shadows

call of the corncrake
screaming of gulls
they are there when you think of them
you are lord of the isles

speed of the running wave

composure of the standing wave

wit of the rippling wave

delight of the breaking wave

a slow release of thistledown

a wide broadcast of thistledown

a light caprice of thistledown

an idle hour of thistledown

a speculative drift of thistledown

at dusk & at dawn

before the day begins
or when the business of the day
is over there are intervals
densities of blue or grey
when you stand on the brink
of a different possibility
a stillness that opens
out into clarity or
a subtlety that folds
back into stillness again
you might almost touch it
an occasion in the air
as steady as a great tree
branching into delicate life

to sit out in the air
and take the shape of the air
its cool spaciousness and precision
and never mind what comes to mind
but attend and cease to attend
remaining cool and spacious
this is the poise of being alone
to be one and no other
and at the same time discover
your shape as a mere integument
that is less a shape than a notion
let it blow away or drop
sitting on a bench in the garden
as the sun goes down or comes up

clinging to willow leaves
clinging to grasses, the mist
disperses and reassembles
alternately masking and revealing
shifting opacities in the dusk
the mist is an insistence
the more tenacious because
it does not insist but gives way
before every advance towards it
closing in again around
whatever ground has been gained
there is no ground to be gained
the clinging mist and the dusk
have erased every advantage

as it sets and rises, the sun
throws light against the canopy
of leaves that spread to contain
its force and to infuse a green
light or glow through the wood
the air has a grain of light
which is almost tangible
but is so evenly distributed
it nowhere waits upon a surface
or sharpens to confuse a form
the space is of light and air
high, neutral, undisturbed
by bird song or by the fire
held behind the screen of leaves

the shadow extends the tree
from substance to possibility
where the tree stands, it walks
while the tree talks, it is silent
it is not a part of the tree
it is not apart from the tree
it comes and goes with the sun
and offers shelter from the sun
the tree is focused in its shadow
at each moment it is at rest
though each moment may be its last
at dawn the shadow is released
and at dusk it will again become
closer to the tree than its name

in the half-light of dusk
after the day has prepared
hard surfaces for inspection
before the night has plunged
things back into themselves
there is a settlement in which
the external and the internal are
continuous with the evening air
if you are alone at the edge
of shadows you are not alone
the hours of light shine in you
with a compacted energy that
also burns in tree and stone
partly revealed and partly veiled

sit for a while on a stone
on the slope above the river
relax and let the light drain
back to the dense tree shadows
before long someone will come
and sit with you on the stone
not beside you but taking up
exactly the space you occupy
it is the one you left behind
on every journey out of yourself
transparent, weighing nothing
breathing with you when you breathe
come to take up residence again
to look out through your eyes

walk for a while beside a river
and beneath the sound of flowing water
or within the sound of flowing water
you will begin to hear or feel
that which does not sound or flow
if you walk alone beside a river
and listen to the sound of rushing water
the haste and the din of rushing water
will stun you into stillness
if you stand for a while beside a river
the little ripples and eddies of water
the whorls and vortices of water
may rob you of the power to move
with any purpose or direction

worked into the texture
of the dusk, into the air
as into a ground, is a reserve
a tone or implication
in which something is withheld
over there where the path
feints in a sepia mist
it flickers, drawn back
briefly into an impatience
of form that is again subsumed
a breath away from emptiness
it is now present with equal
tension throughout a locality
that it gathers from the air

at dawn and at dusk the pools
the little pools are lakes
that ripple out and hold
fractured and reformed images
that drop into a larger dimension
dark cloud and darker tree
confuse with baroque contours
the place where earth meets water
where leaf canopy becomes sky
and one who was passing by
has been detained by distances
that might be heights or depths
earth, water, air or fire
in a break on a stretch of moor

as longing stretches out
and begins to detach itself from
the initial object of longing
it becomes present everywhere
and can be found in everything
forming and informing everything
the weight of this stone is longing
the curve of that tree is longing
and longing makes the lightest breeze
sigh in the tall dead bracken
longing is not for this or that
but is longing for itself alone
to know itself in late afternoon
longing is a kind of lingering

a bird so light it can arrive
the same moment as the morning
weighing little more than a shadow
suddenly on the highest branch
to rest at the top of its impulse
without disturbing a leaf
hardly bending the light
with the plain shape of a leaf
but more detached from the branch
it can drop through the tree
through a play of shadows
and as suddenly rise
without the aid of a breeze
where a leaf can only fall

do you know the land

when the mist lifts
a mist of bog cotton
lingers on the moor

a few tattered banners
as if skeins of mist
snagged on the grass

in wool and in cloud
among bog asphodels
bog cotton grows

a conspicuous plant
of wet moorland
of bogs and bog pools

the seed head droops
into shining white tufts
or silky tassels

that hang in the air
that are lashed by the wind
that dance on the breeze

sheep and deer graze
red grouse browse
bog cotton grass

it is a suspension of belief
a flag of truce
a slow snow

an easterly or ecstacy
coursing through it
does not change it

the cotton grass way
is to hover over
the information

it is at a strange
distance always
however near

best go alone
over the carbon sink
through the sundews

at loch grinneabhat

sandpiper piping from a stone
   lifting and lighting
on the same stone
   piping on alone

lighting and lifting
   out over the loch
in a turn or sally
   a swift sortie

small mechanical toy
   prompted by a signal
remote from itself
   to circle round itself

walks or runs on ground
   wades in water
will perch on low objects
   bobbing head and tail

constantly bobbing head and tail
   flight note a shrill wee twee
by hill lochs by sea lochs
   sporadically by lowland waters

flies low over water
   shrill call and flickering wings
a display for no one
   note heard by stone

will preach from low objects
   turning and returning
to the same theme
   in the half-light in the same tone

a few variations
   on an original air
strong agogic accents
   elaborate grace notes

its pipe is its throat
   the little music
stopped with gammarids
   worms and larvae

dark along the peat haggs
   behind bog cotton
a bleary chink of light
   flickering and throbbing

within the visual field
   you do not occur
lost or taken up with
   what happens to be there

out over a waste
   of dusk again it tries
its circuit brief
   as ripple or dapple

lullaby

brindled cow and dun cow
from the field by the lochan
in the glow of the evening
come quietly home

the belted galloways
from the rough pasture
through the course grasses
come quietly home

the young red bull
drunk on clover
over the machair
brought quietly home

the four fresians
laden with milk
knowing the way
come quietly home

dusk

a wide landscape
in pen and ink
pencil and chalk
with chinese white
on grey paper

a fine impression
on laid paper
a few stains
in the lower margin
slight surface dirt

watercolour
with pencil
pen and ink
heavily-laden
apple tree

brown wash
over pencil
pen and ink
on discoloured paper
some rubbing out

three words

the spaces of dusk
the spaces of twilight
the spaces of evening

the fires of dusk
the fires of twilight
the fires of evening

the shelter of dusk
the shelter of twilight
the shelter of evening

the shores of dusk
the shores of twilight
the shores of evening

taking the long shore road home

friendship

ACKNOWLEDGEMENTS

With thanks to *Poetical Histories*, *Morning Star*, *Longhouse*, Arc Publications, Polygon and Moschatel Press where these poems first appeared.